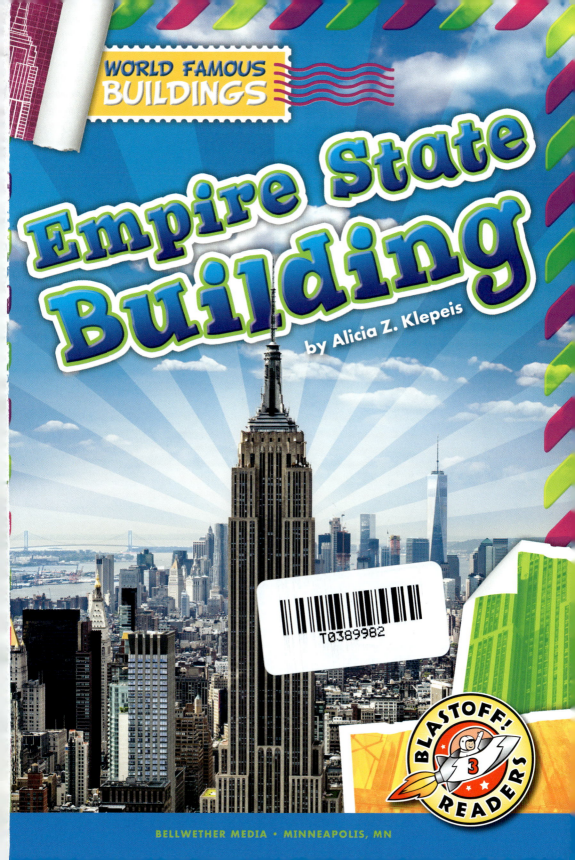

Blastoff! Readers are carefully developed by literacy experts to build reading stamina and move students toward fluency by combining standards-based content with developmentally appropriate text.

Level 1 provides the most support through repetition of high-frequency words, light text, predictable sentence patterns, and strong visual support.

Level 2 offers early readers a bit more challenge through varied sentences, increased text load, and text-supportive special features.

Level 3 advances early-fluent readers toward fluency through increased text load, less reliance on photos, advancing concepts, longer sentences, and more complex special features.

★ **Blastoff! Universe**

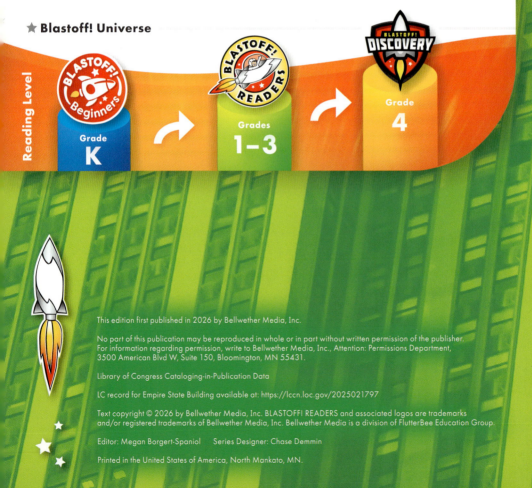

This edition first published in 2026 by Bellwether Media, Inc.

No part of this publication may be reproduced in whole or in part without written permission of the publisher. For information regarding permission, write to Bellwether Media, Inc., Attention: Permissions Department, 3500 American Blvd W, Suite 150, Bloomington, MN 55431.

Library of Congress Cataloging-in-Publication Data

LC record for Empire State Building available at: https://lccn.loc.gov/2025021797

Text copyright © 2026 by Bellwether Media, Inc. BLASTOFF! READERS and associated logos are trademarks and/or registered trademarks of Bellwether Media, Inc. Bellwether Media is a division of FlutterBee Education Group.

Editor: Megan Borgert-Spaniol   Series Designer: Chase Demmin

Printed in the United States of America, North Mankato, MN.

Table of Contents

What Is the Empire State Building?	4
History of the Empire State Building	8
Parts of the Empire State Building	14
The Empire State Building Today	18
Glossary	22
To Learn More	23
Index	24

What Is the Empire State Building?

New York City

The Empire State Building is a tall tower. It is in New York City, New York.

It was the world's tallest building for about 40 years. It was also the first to have more than 100 floors!

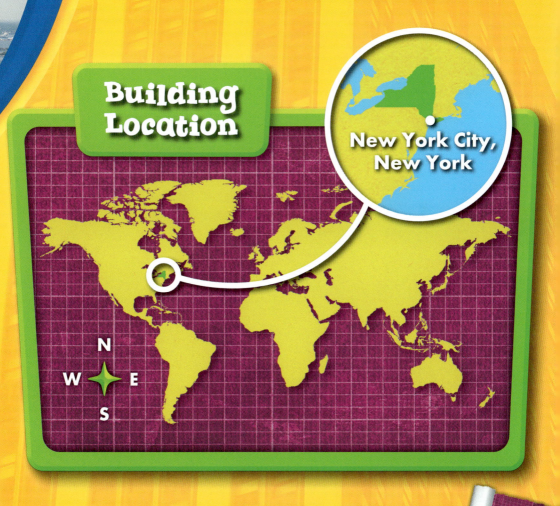

Building Location

New York City, New York

The Empire State Building has restaurants, shops, and hundreds of offices.

observation deck

Many visitors see the building. They can visit a museum. They look out from the tower's **observation decks**.

History of the Empire State Building

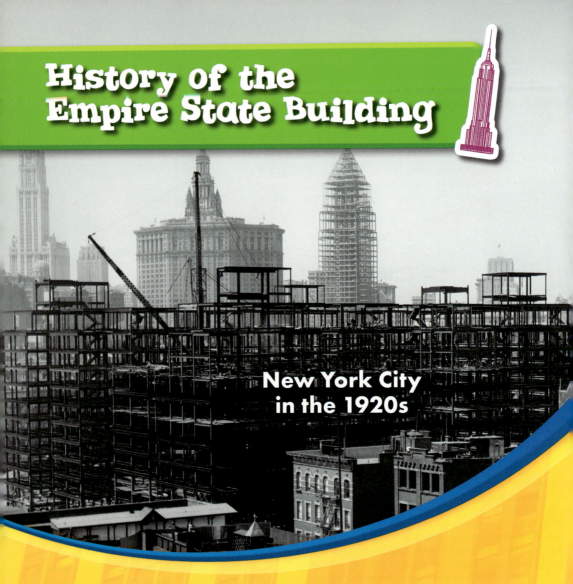

New York City in the 1920s

New York City grew in the 1920s. Many towers were being built. Businessman John J. Raskob wanted his to be the tallest.

John worked with **architect** William F. Lamb. William drew the tower's **design** in two weeks!

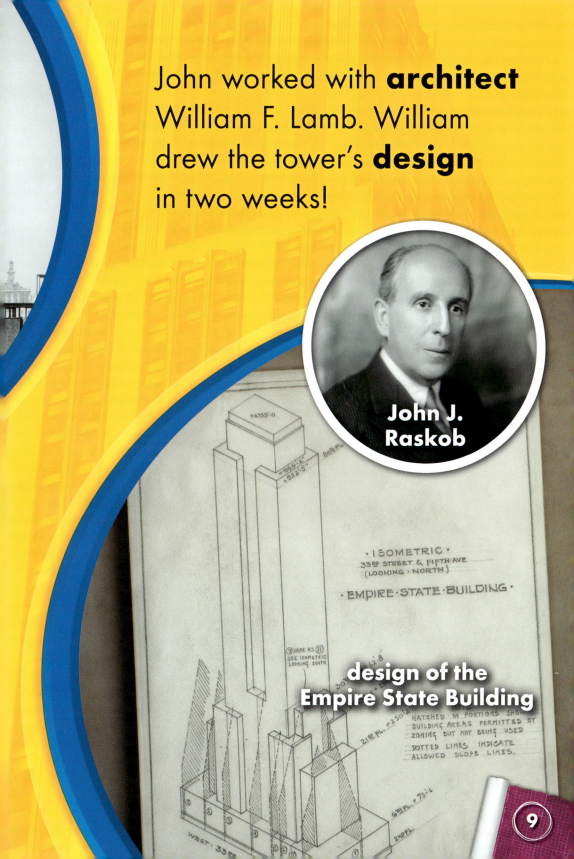

John J. Raskob

design of the Empire State Building

Work began in 1930. The building was finished in 1931.

Building it was hard work. Crews dug into the ground with **steam shovels**. Then they built the **foundation** with steel and **concrete**.

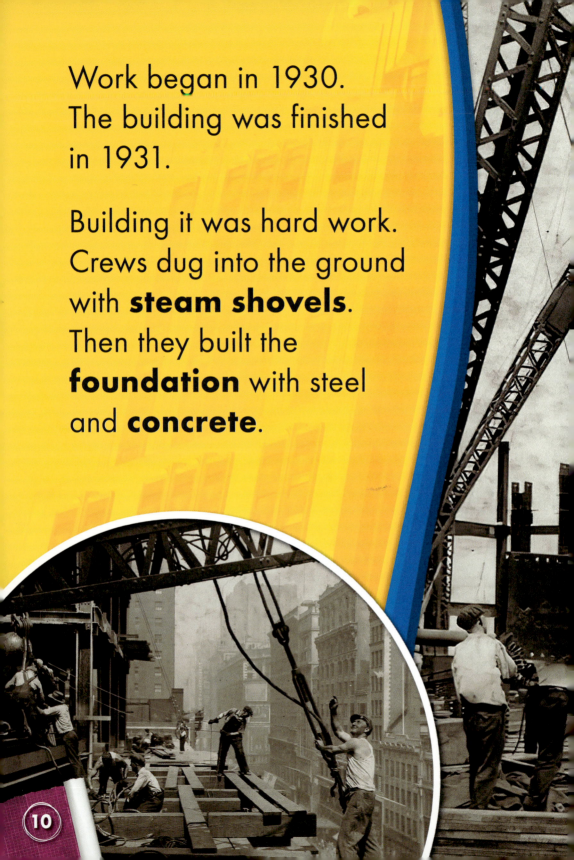

Crews used cranes to lift steel beams for the building's frame. They joined the beams together with **rivets**.

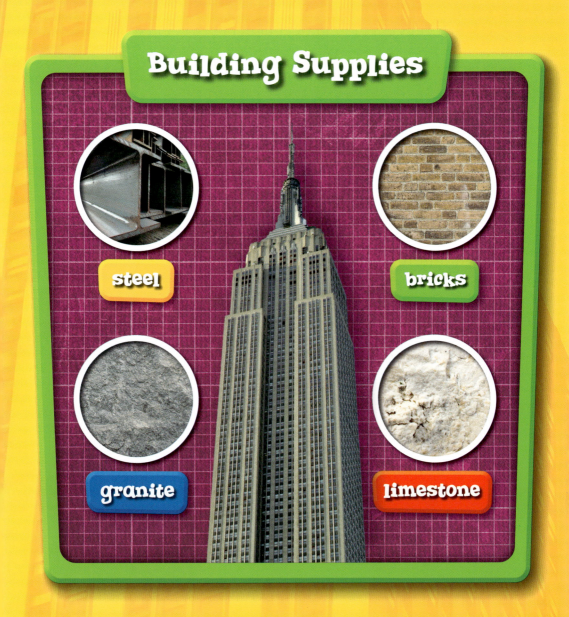

The outside of the building was made with 10 million bricks! Crews covered the bricks with granite and limestone.

Parts of the Empire State Building

The Empire State Building has an **art deco** style. The building narrows as it rises. This lets light and air reach the streets below.

Inside, the **lobby** features an art deco **mural**.

lobby

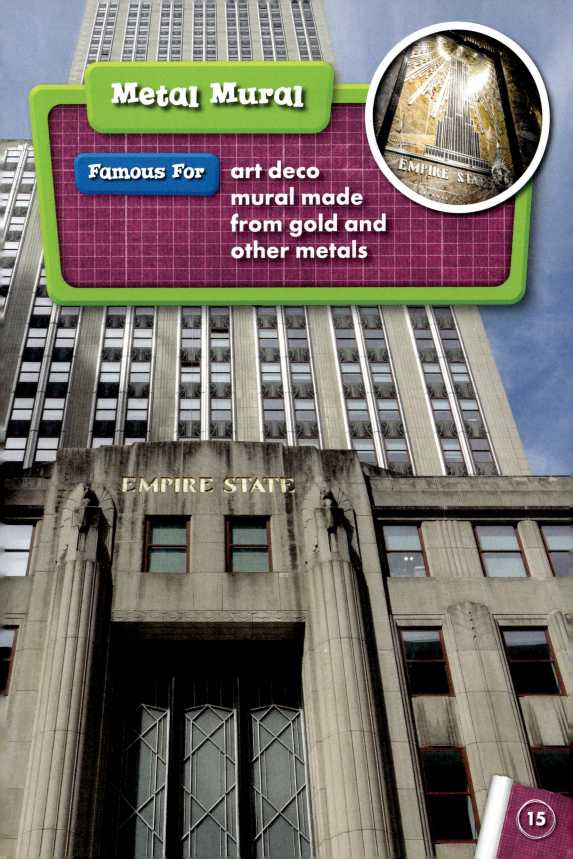

Metal Mural

Famous For art deco mural made from gold and other metals

The Empire State Building is 1,454 feet (443 meters) tall! This includes the **spire** and **antenna**.

The highest public observation deck is 102 floors up! It offers views up to 80 miles (129 kilometers) away!

The Empire State Building Today

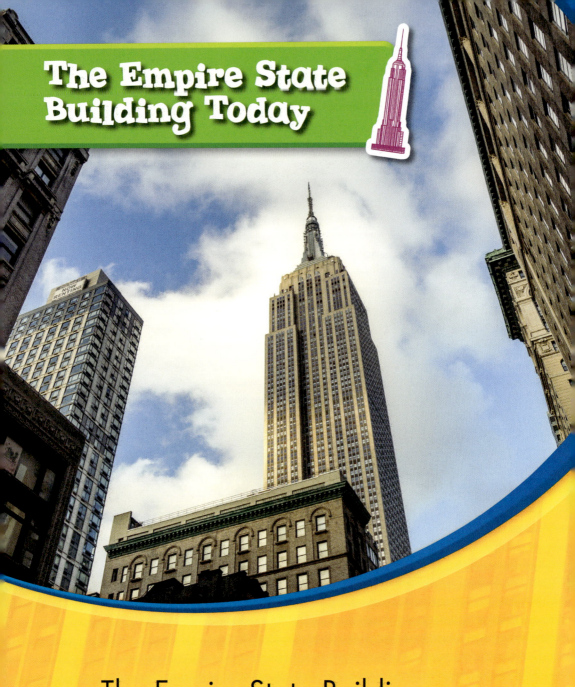

The Empire State Building has changed over time.

Today, all the windows have a special coating. This helps the building use less **energy** to heat and cool it.

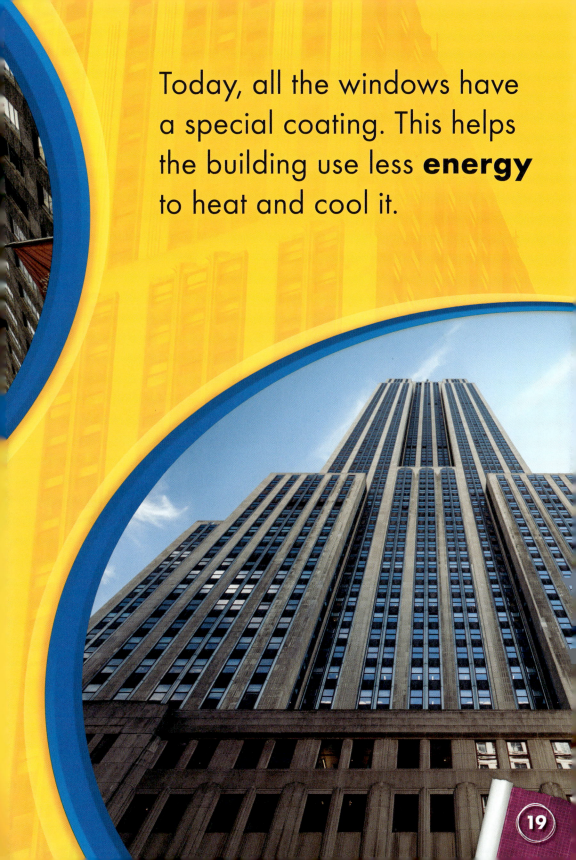

Since 2012, the building has been lit with **LED lights**. They can light the building with millions of colors!

More than 2.5 million visitors go to the Empire State Building each year. Many more enjoy the building from far away!

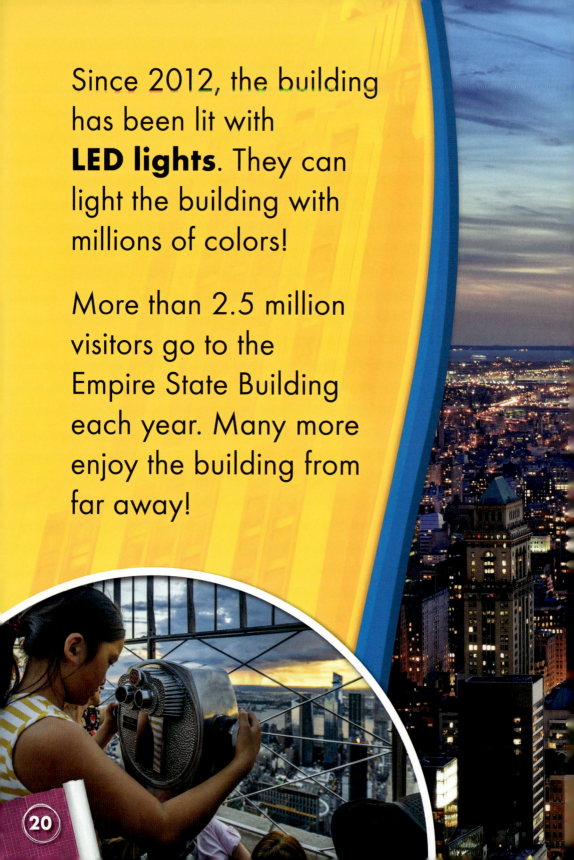

Glossary

antenna—a rod, wire, or other device used to send and receive radio or TV signals

architect—a person who designs and plans buildings

art deco—related to a design style popular in the 1920s and 1930s; art deco is marked by bold outlines, geometric shapes, and modern materials.

concrete—a hard, strong building material made with cement, sand, rocks, and water

design—a plan for a building, object, or pattern

energy—the power to make things work

foundation—the base or support on which a building rests

LED lights—lights that use less energy than older types of light bulbs

lobby—an entry hall or room that often serves as a waiting area

mural—a large work of art on a wall or ceiling

observation decks—platforms built so that people can look out at a view

rivets—short metal bolts or pins used to hold two pieces of metal together

spire—a pointed structure at the top of a building

steam shovels—digging machines that are powered by steam

To Learn More

AT THE LIBRARY

LaRoche, Amelia. *New York City: History, People, Landmarks: Central Park, Empire State Building, Ellis Island*. Mount Joy, Pa.: Curious Fox Books, 2024.

Leaf, Christina. *New York City*. Minneapolis, Minn.: Bellwether Media, 2024.

Mahoney, Emily Jankowski. *20 Fun Facts About the Empire State Building*. New York, N.Y.: Gareth Stevens Publishing, 2020.

ON THE WEB

FACTSURFER

Factsurfer.com gives you a safe, fun way to find more information.

1. Go to www.factsurfer.com.

2. Enter "Empire State Building" into the search box and click 🔍.

3. Select your book cover to see a list of related content.

Index

antenna, 16
architect, 9
art deco style, 14
beams, 12
bricks, 13
building location, 5
building supplies, 13
concrete, 10
cranes, 12
crews, 10, 12, 13
design, 9
energy, 19
floors, 5, 17
foundation, 10
frame, 12
granite, 13
history, 5, 8, 9, 10, 12, 13, 20
Lamb, William F., 9
LED lights, 20, 21
limestone, 13
lobby, 14

mural, 14, 15
museum, 7
New York City, New York, 4, 5, 8
observation decks, 7, 17
offices, 6
Raskob, John J., 8, 9
restaurants, 6
rivets, 12
shape, 14
shops, 6
size, 4, 5, 8, 16, 17
spire, 16
steam shovels, 10
steel, 10, 12
views, 17
visitors, 7, 20
windows, 19

The images in this book are reproduced through the courtesy of: Oscity, front cover, p. 4; Deliris, front cover (inset), background (throughout); pisaphotography, front cover (inset); LittleDraw, icon (throughout); peresanz, p. 3; Patti McConville/ Alamy Stock Photo, p. 6; starmaro, p. 7; Keystone View Company/ FPG/ Archive Photos/ Getty Images, p. 8; Harris & Ewing Photographs/ Library of Congress, p. 9 (inset); Shreve, Lamb & Harmon/ Wikimedia, p. 9; American Photo Archive/ Alamy Stock Photo, pp. 10, 10-11, 12; Marianoblanco, p. 13; sawaeng wonglakorn, p. 13 (steel); Bits and Splits, p. 13 (bricks); mvdesign, p. 13 (granite); vvoe, p. 13 (limestone); EWY Media, p. 14; Joaquin Ossorio Castillo, p. 15 (inset); OliverFoerstner, pp. 14-15, 18; travelview, pp. 16-17; Einar Magnus Magnusson, p. 19; Ondrej Bucek, p. 20; Songquan Deng, pp. 20-21; Tupungato, p. 23.

24